IGUANODON

by Janet Riehecky
illustrated by Diana Magnuson

THE CHILD'S WORLD

MANKATO, MN

*Grateful appreciation is expressed to Bret S. Beall,
Curatorial Coordinator for the Department of Geology,
Field Museum of Natural History, Chicago, Illinois,
who reviewed this book to insure its accuracy.*

PAPERBACK EDITION
ISBN 0-516-46253-9

Library of Congress Cataloging in Publication Data

Riehecky, Janet, 1953-
  Iguanodon / by Janet Riehecky ; illustrated by Diana Magnuson.
    p. cm. — (Dinosaurs)
  Summary: Describes the physical characteristics, habits, and
natural environment of the plant-eating Iguanodon.
  ISBN 0-89565-544-6
  1. Iguanodon—Juvenile literature. [1. Iguanodon.
2. Dinosaurs.] I. Magnuson, Diana. II. Title. III. Series:
Riehecky, Janet, 1953-   Dinosaur books.
QE862.065R53   1989
567.9'7—dc20   89-15850
                                  CIP
                                   AC

IGUANODON

Long ago the earth was filled with
dinosaurs. When they all died, they left
behind many clues about themselves.

Scientists have concluded some interesting things from studying these clues.

For instance, scientists think horned dinosaurs fought each other to see who would be the leader of a herd.

And they think that "bone-heads" (dinosaurs with very thick skulls) banged their heads together for the same reason.

Some scientists think that one type of
dinosaur had trouble getting up if it fell
down.

And they also think that another type
watched over its babies much as a mother
bird does today.

One of the first types of dinosaurs scientists learned about was the Iguanodon (ig-WAN-oh-don). We now know that the Iguanodon was an average-sized dinosaur that walked on its back legs and had a sharp spike on each of its front feet. But in 1822, when it was first discovered, scientists didn't know it was a dinosaur. They didn't even know that dinosaurs had ever existed.

Iguanodon was discovered when a woman named Mary Ann Mantell found some enormous teeth in a pile of gravel. She showed them to her husband, Dr. Gideon Algernon Mantell, who was interested in fossils. He studied the teeth and showed them to some experts. He learned that the teeth looked like those of the iguana lizard—but they were much, much larger.

Dr. Mantell went to the pit that the gravel had come from. There he found more teeth and a few giant bones. He decided they must have belonged to a huge relative of the iguana. He named the huge reptile Iguanodon, which means "iguana tooth." Nobody knew it yet, but dinosaurs had been discovered.

Many scientists began looking for giant reptile bones—and they found them. Giant bones had been found before, but scientists thought they were the bones of known animals, such as elephants. Now they realized that they belonged to huge reptiles that were no longer on earth. They

learned that many different kinds of giant
reptiles had once lived on earth.

One scientist pictured in his mind what
he thought those huge reptiles might have
looked like. The picture was so frightening
he gave the reptiles the name "dinosaur,"
which means "terrible lizard."

Some scientists studied the bones of the Iguanodon which were found by Dr. Mantell and others. They tried to figure out how they went together. It was like trying to put together a jigsaw puzzle with only half the pieces. Scientists made a life-sized model of what they thought the Iguanodon was like. The dinosaur looked something like a fat rhinoceros with scales. They even put the spike from one of the front feet on the creature's nose!

The scientists were very anxious to show the world their dinosaur. (They didn't know they had made so many mistakes.) So, when the model was half done, they decided to have a dinner party—in the dinosaur!

Many important scientists were invited. They were a bit crowded, but everyone had a wonderful time. There was excellent food and many a toast. This was probably the only time in history that a dinner was inside a dinosaur without being the dinosaur's dinner!

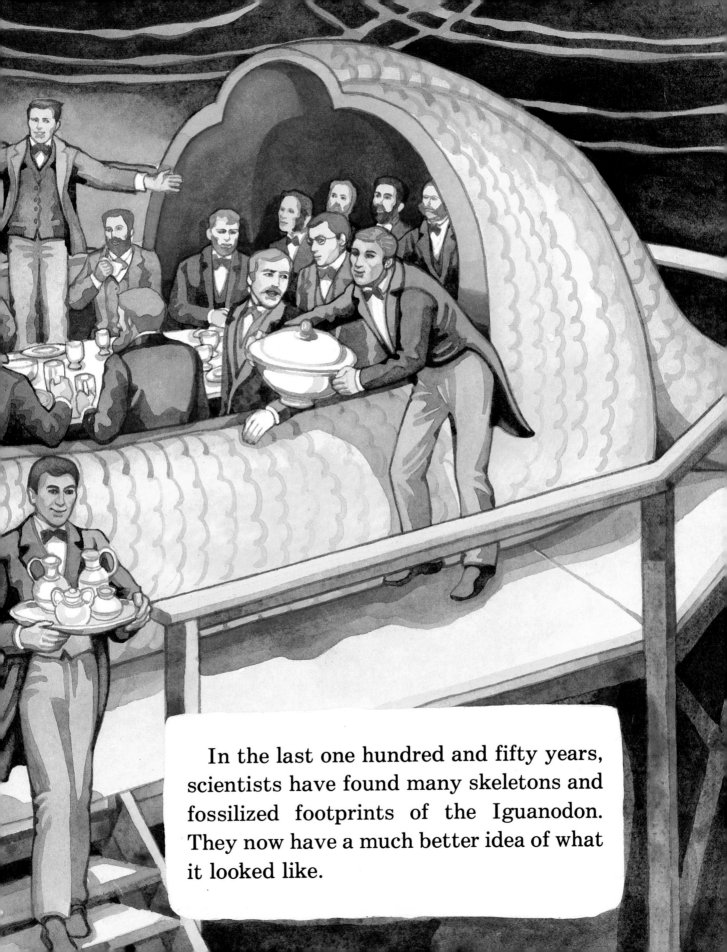

In the last one hundred and fifty years, scientists have found many skeletons and fossilized footprints of the Iguanodon. They now have a much better idea of what it looked like.

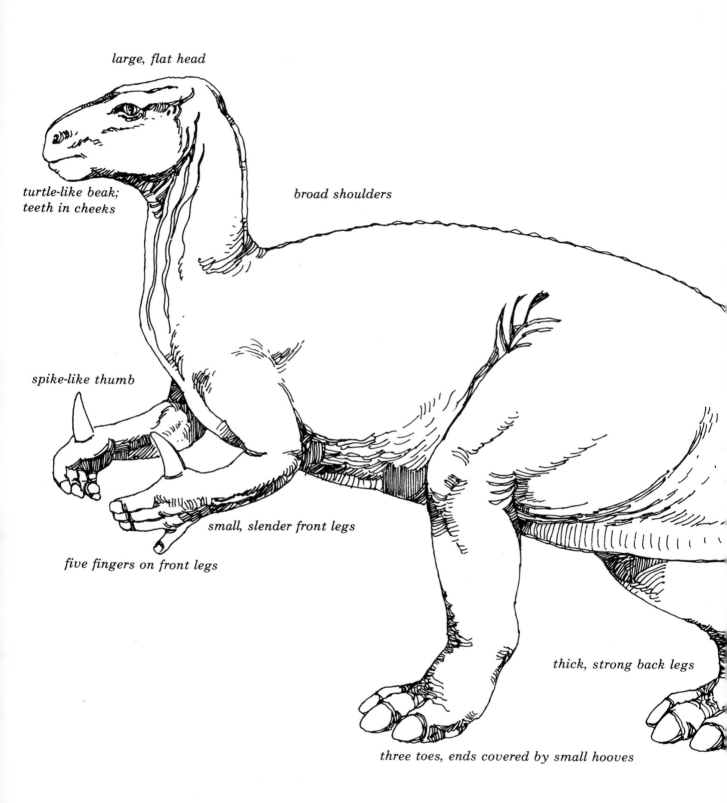

large, flat head

turtle-like beak;
teeth in cheeks

broad shoulders

spike-like thumb

small, slender front legs

five fingers on front legs

thick, strong back legs

three toes, ends covered by small hooves

The Iguanodon was about thirty-three feet long, about fifteen feet tall, and weighed about three tons. An Iguanodon walked on its strong back legs with its tail stretched out stiffly behind for balance. The front of its body was bent low. (It looked something like a fat kangaroo!) When it wanted to stretch up high to nibble some tree leaves or just wanted to rest awhile, it reared up and sat on the base of its tail.

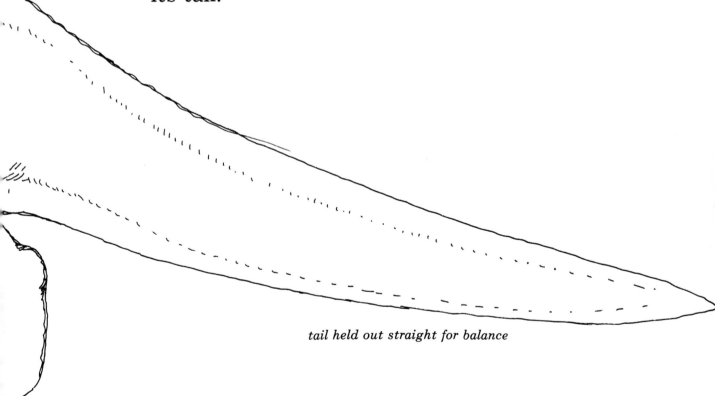

tail held out straight for balance

The Iguanodon was a plant-eating dinosaur. It had a large mouth with a horny, turtle-like beak. There were no teeth in the front of its mouth, but in its cheeks it had about a hundred. The teeth were slanted so that the upper teeth slid along the outside of the lower teeth when the Iguanodon closed its mouth, sort of like scissors closing.

Some scientists think the Iguanodon had a long tongue which it could wrap around reeds and ferns. It would then pull them into its mouth and swallow them. And if, by accident, some small branches or tough roots came along, the Iguanodon could crunch them in its scissor-like teeth, instead of showing bad manners and spitting them out.

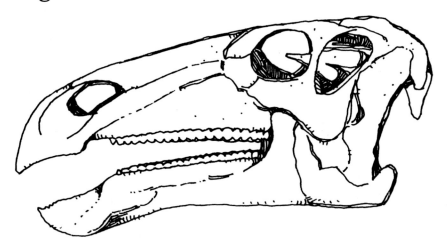

One of the most unusual things about the Iguanodon was that it had a spike on each front foot. It had five "fingers," just as people do, but not even Captain Hook had a spike like Iguanodon's!

The three fingers in the middle of the Iguanodon's hand were rather stiff. They bent more easily backward than forward. The finger on the outside bent like a human finger. It may have been used to grab food. But in place of a thumb, the Iguanodon had a long, sharp spike, like a gangster's knife. The spike was ten inches long. On top of that was a sixteen-inch claw! Now, that was a wicked weapon!

The Iguanodon probably used its thumb as a gangster uses his knife—to slash at an attacker. It could have punctured the thickest hide.

And, no doubt about it, there were dino-saurs that wanted to attack Iguanodon. Many fierce meat-eating dinosaurs lived in the same area at the same time. Two of the worst, Megalosaurus and Altispinax, were relatives of Tyrannosaurus. Alti-spinax was a strange-looking creature with a sail on its back.

The Iguanodon could fight if it needed
to, but it seldom needed to. It had sharp
eyes (the better to see a meat eater sneak-
ing up), good ears (the better to hear one
coming), and a wonderful nose (the better
to smell trouble). It also had a large brain,
so it was smart enough to find the best
escape route.

Iguanodon also protected itself from meat eaters by traveling in large herds. The herds roamed the swampy countryside, wading through marshes, looking for food. Some scientists think the Iguanodon lived in water part of the time. Even if it didn't, it could escape into a lake or stream when threatened by a meat-eating dinosaur.

Scientists don't know much about how the Iguanodon had babies. They think it laid eggs and that it may have taken care of the babies while the babies were young. However, this is an area where scientists still have a lot to learn.

The whole story of dinosaurs is not yet told. Each new discovery adds new clues, but always there is more to learn about those "terrible lizards"—the dinosaurs!

 **Dinosaur Fun**

You can make your own dinosaur model with homemade play dough. (But you'll have to make an extra-big batch if you want to have a dinner party in your dinosaur model!)

You will need:

— 1 cup flour
— ⅓ cup salt
— about ½ cup water (or less)
— a few drops of vegetable oil
— food coloring

1. Stir the flour and salt together in a bowl.
2. Add the food coloring and oil to the water. Then *slowly* pour the water, a little at a time, into the flour and salt, mixing with your hands. If the dough gets too sticky, add more flour.
3. Knead the dough until you are sure it is mixed well. Try shaping the dough into an Iguanodon or another dinosaur!